The American Flag

by Judith Jango-Cohen

 Lerner Publications Company • Minneapolis

To my "big brother" Leonard, with whom I love to talk politics

The author wishes to thank Marilyn Zoidis, curator of the Star-Spangled Banner project at the Smithsonian Institution's National Museum of American History.

Text copyright © 2004 by Judith Jango-Cohen

This book is available in two editions:
Library binding by Lerner Publications Company, a division of Lerner Publishing Group
Soft cover by First Avenue Editions, an imprint of Lerner Publishing Group
241 First Avenue North
Minneapolis, MN 55401 U.S.A.

Website address: www.lernerbooks.com

Words in **bold type** are explained in a glossary on page 31.

Library of Congress Cataloging-in-Publication Data

Jango-Cohen, Judith.
    The American flag / by Judith Jango-Cohen.
        p.   cm. – (Pull ahead books)
    Summary: Shows what various flags of the United States have meant,
and what the Stars and Stripes means to us today.
    ISBN: 0–8225–3804–0 (lib. bdg. : alk. paper)
    ISBN: 0–8225–3753–2 (pbk. : alk. paper)
    1. Flags–United States–Juvenile literature. [1. Flags–United States.]
I. Title. II. Series.
CR113 .J36 2004
929.9'2'0973–dc21   2002013948

Manufactured in the United States of America
1 2 3 4 5 6 – DP – 09 08 07 06 05 04

Whose red, white, and blue flag is this?

This is the first American flag. Each
stripe stood for one **colony**. There
were 13 American colonies.

The crosses stood for **Great Britain**.
The flag showed that the American
colonies were part of Great Britain.

By 1776, the American colonies did not
want to be ruled by Great Britain. They
had to fight a war for their freedom.

During the war, the United States of America became a new country. A flag with British crosses was not a good **symbol** for America anymore.

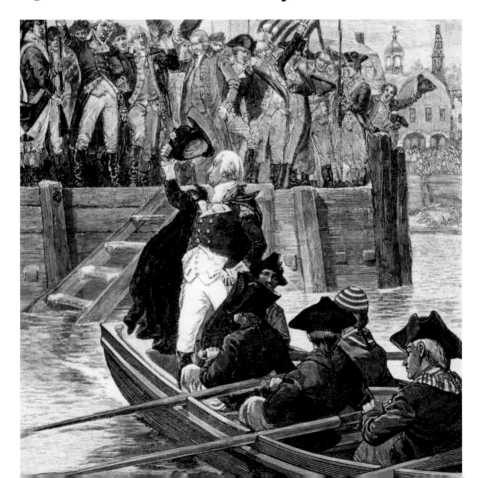

America chose a new symbol on June 14, 1777. This flag's 13 stars and 13 stripes stood for the 13 **states** in the United States.

American ships flew this new flag.
They flew it in battles with the British.
Finally, the United States won the war.

In 1795, the United States needed a new flag. Count its stars and stripes.

The United States had 15 states in
1795. The new flag had one star and
one stripe for each state.

This flag was flying in the War of 1812. America was fighting Great Britain again. A poet named Francis Scott Key watched one of the battles.

Key watched the **Stars and Stripes** wave. The British would take down the American flag if they won the battle.

The next day, the flag was still waving. The United States had won. Key was so happy and proud that he wrote a poem.

His poem became the words to the
national anthem. This song is called
"The Star-Spangled Banner."

America added five stars to its
Star-Spangled Banner in 1818. It
took away two stripes.

The 13 stripes stood for the first 13 states. Each star stood for a state in the United States.

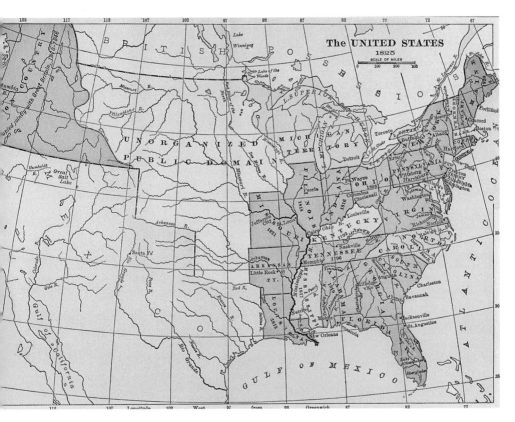

The United States grew bigger. More
stars were added. In 1912, the flag
had 48 stars for 48 states.

This flag flew through World War I and
World War II.

Alaska and Hawaii were the last states to add stars to the flag. Alaska's star went up in 1959. Hawaii added its star in 1960.

Now the flag has 13 broad stripes. It has 50 bright stars. Where do you see the Stars and Stripes?

Americans carry the flag in parades.

They carry the flag in marches.

The flag flies when people from other countries become Americans.

It flies when we honor those who fought for our country.

The flag flies when we sing the national
anthem. We put our hands over our
hearts. We look at the flag.

The American flag is a symbol of the
United States. Look around your town.
Where is the flag flying near you?

About the American Flag

■ Betsy Ross sewed flags, but no one really knows if she made the first American flag.

■ A sea captain first called the flag "Old Glory" in the early 1800s. During the Civil War, he hid Old Glory inside a quilt.

■ In 1892, Francis Bellamy wrote, "I pledge allegiance to my Flag and the Republic for which it stands—one nation indivisible—with liberty and justice for all." Schoolchildren first recited the pledge on October 12, 1892. It was the 400th anniversary of Columbus's arrival in America.

■ Robert Peary was the first person to reach the North Pole. He left an American flag there in 1909.

■ Neil Armstrong was the first person to walk on the Moon. He left an American flag there in 1969.

■ The flag flies at the White House when the president is there.

Rules for Displaying the Flag

- The flag should never touch anything below it, like the floor or the ground.

- The flag should be flown at night only if it is lit up.

- The flag should never be used as clothing.

- Only all-weather flags should be flown in bad weather.

- The flag should be flown in or near every school during the school day.

- When the flag is hung on a wall or window, the stars should appear in the upper left-hand corner to the viewer.

- The flag should not be printed on paper napkins, boxes, or anything that is made to be used and thrown away.

- Flag pins should be worn on the left side of the chest, near the heart.

More about the American Flag

Books

Key, Francis Scott. *The Star-Spangled Banner.* New York: Bantam Doubleday Dell, 1992.

Swanson, June. *I Pledge Allegiance.* Minneapolis: Carolrhoda Books, 2002.

Wallner, Alexandra. *Betsy Ross.* New York: Holiday House, 1994.

Websites

The Betsy Ross Homepage
<http://www.ushistory.org/betsy/>

The Flag of the United States
<http://www.usflag.org/>

Flag of the United States of America
<http://www.geocities.com/CapitolHill/4182/>

A Guide to American Flags
<http://www.law.ou.edu/hist/flags/>

Visiting the American Flag

You can see the flag that Francis Scott Key was watching before he wrote the words to our national anthem. It is on display at the National Museum of American History in Washington, D.C. See their website: <http://americanhistory.si.edu/ssb/>

Glossary

colony: an area that is settled by people from another place. This settlement is ruled by the country the people came from.

Great Britain: a country in Europe that ruled settlements in America. Great Britain is made up of England, Northern Ireland, Scotland, and Wales.

national anthem: a song that praises a country. It is a symbol of that county.

Stars and Stripes: a nickname for the American flag

states: areas with their own governments that joined together to form the United States of America

symbol: an object that stands for an idea, a country, or a person

Index

Photo Acknowledgments

The pictures in this book have been reproduced with the permission of: © North Wind Picture Archives, pp. 3, 7, 9, 12, 17; © New England Life Insurance Company, p. 4; Library of Congress, pp. 5, 6, 8, 14; © N. Carter/North Wind Picture Archives, p. 10; © Bettmann/CORBIS, pp. 11, 13; © Chuck Savage/CORBIS, p. 15; © Todd Strand/Independent Picture Service, pp. 16, 18; National Archives, p. 19; Photodisc, pp. 20, 26; EyeWire, p. 21; © Jeffrey Greenberg/Visuals Unlimited, pp. 22, 24, 25; © Joe McDonald/Visuals Unlimited, p. 23; © John Sohlden/Visuals Unlimited, p. 27.

Cover photo used with the permission of Corbis Royalty Free Images.

1903